WORDS
OF THE
BROKEN

WORDS
OF THE
BROKEN

FELICIA GRUBBS

ARPress

ARPress
45 Dan Road Suite 5
Canton MA 02021

Hotline: 1(800) 220-7660
Fax: 1(855) 752-6001

Ordering Information:
Quantity sales. Special discounts are available on quantity purchases by corporations, associations, and others. For details, contact the publisher at the address above.

Printed in the United States of America.

ISBN-13:	Paperback	979-8-89389-614-5
	eBook	979-8-89389-615-2

Library of Congress Control Number: 2024921306

Contents

Growing up I was Always Heard

Growing up I was always heard.
Everyone has a purpose, everyone has a reason.
Everyone is good at something, everyone is good for something.
Have you ever looked in a mirror and asked
"What am I good for? Why am I here? What is my purpose?"
Have you ever felt like you are not good enough?
Ever felt like no matter what you say or do, it's still not good enough?
Then you ask yourself" why am I not good enough?
Why am I the blame for everything? Why am I always wrong?"
Why am I here? Nothing about me matter's to anyone?
Why no one wants me around?
Then ask yourself "Am I really that bad of a person that no one wants me around?"
Why is it so easy for everyone to dismiss me?
Ever thought you was the only one with these thoughts?
Well you not. Others have these thought.
They just won't admit it.
And if asked they look at you like you said something unforgivable. Then tell you well of course I don't think like that. What's wrong with you. Asking me something like that…
Just try and remember you are not alone.
You are good enough
You have a purpose and you have a reason.

Be Cautious

Just a word of caution.
When angry be cautious.
The hurtful words
That you have spoken
Will always be
Cause they can
Never be unspoken
You can not go back in time
To unbreak the heart
That your spoken words
Has torn apart.
   Spoken Words
      Tragically leaves
         Shattered Hearts!!

Can't Please Everyone

Life is rough. Life is also tough.
No matter who you are.
No matter what you say or do.
No matter how you act.
Somewhere someone will always have something to say about it.
Someone will always have some kind of remark to make you feel bad.
About what you said or done.
Try not to let them bring you down.
Always remember you are not here to please anyone but yourself.
Can't Always Please Everyone
No matter how hard you try
There will always be some kind of comment about what you did or said.
No matter how hard you try, no matter what you say or do.
You just can't please everyone.
There will always be someone that will have something bad to say about you.
So try to remember......
No one is perfect. Everyone has faults.
People will bring up your faults....
In hopes that there's will not be seen.
Meanwhile they are pointing a finger at you.
They do not seem to realize that the whole time
they pointing at you
They have 3 fingers pointing back at them.

Emptiness

There is a whole in my heart
That will always be
An emptiness longing to be filled
Even though it could never be
Every since the day you were taken from me

Everyone Breaks Eventually

Mental and verbal abuse has away of breaking down everyone.
Even the strong willed and the unbreakable; eventually breaks.
When they have been mentally and verbally abused for years.
From then on; they have a constant battle; a constant struggle
everyday
To block out the hurtful things that made them that way
When you have a broken mind you find out quick
That others no longer want you around because now you are
different.
They don't know how to deal with you anymore. So they push
you so far away you start believing you are all alone

Everyone Hurts

Everyone has pain
Everyone hurts
No two people
Will deal with
Things the same
Everyone has their way
To deal with pain.
Some deal with
Things with ease
While others find it
More difficult to do
The same

Give it Time

They say. Just give it time
Time heals everything.
Then you realize'; it's just a lie
Time does not heal everything
Time just teaches!
Teaches you how to hide the pain
Teaches you how
To hide your feelings
In time you learn…..
To be cheerful…..
When you want to cry
To smile when…..
When you want to scream
Teaches you to be around others.
When you just want to be alone
In time you learn to hide everything
From everyone
So no one ssee's your pain

Life and Death

Life leads to love
Love leads to pain
Pain leads to hate
Hate leads to destruction
Destruction leads to death

Miss You More and More

I miss you more and more
With each passing day
Wish I could see you
Just one more time.
But we both know
Even that would not do.
You already knew
The hardest thing
For me to do would be
To tell you goodbye
For the last and final time
I miss you more and more
With each passing day
Hoping that one day
The ache in my heart will go away.
But I now realize that
Will always be an ache in my heart
Every since you got taken away
From me

Pain Changes Everyone

It's a hard situation
When you feel so alone
It's a bad situation
When you don't
Let anyone in
It's a sad situation
When you trust no one
When you have been let down so much.
By the very ones who says
I'll be there for you
The wounds that causes
Is deep and is everlasting

Pain does damage
No one can see
Damaging pain that last
For all eternity
Damaging pain changes you.
Once you feel this kind of pain
You won't ever be the same

Painful Situation

It's a sad and painful situation.
When your brain is broken.
There is nothing you can do you can't call the doctor and say
"hey doc let's schedule that brain surgery.
I need a new brain. The one I got is broken"
They do not do brain transplants yet.
When you are constantly mentally,and verbally abused.
To the point your brain is actually broken.
The only thing you can do is learn to deal with it.
No matter how you deal with it,
You will never be the same.
You will always be reminded of the cruel, mean and hateful
things you were told.
All ways a reminder of what you have been through.
And now you are permanently damaged.
Damaged from within, where no one can see
Damage from the worst kind of abuse.
A broken bone will heal; a bruise will go away.
But a broken mind will always remain.

Silent Tears

The worst tears
Are the silent ones.
They are caused by people
Who tell you they love you
The people who tell you
They would never hurt you.
Those people cause
The worst pain
Those people cause
Silent Tears
Silent Tears linger
For all eternity
They come and go
Like a whisper
To let you know
They still here.
Silent Tears can't
Be explained to most
But to some;
No need to explain
Cause they know the pain
Silent Tears are shown to some
By the glimpse of an eye
Silent Tears changes you
Most don't understand why

You try to explain
And realize it's no use
Cause unless people experience
Silent Tears
They will never know why
Silent Tears come and go
Like a whisper
To remind you
They will always remain
Causing never ending pain
That can't be explained
For those who has
Silent Tears
Try to remember
You are not to blame
For your silent tears
That forever will remain

Spoken Words

Words are a weapon
When used to cause pain.
Be careful what you say
Cause once they are spoken
Things are not the same.
Don't use words
To hurt the one you love

Words always linger and remain
Long after thee heart aches and pains.
Spoken Words cut deep
And the wounds that area left behind
Truly never heal.
    Those wounds will always remain
       Causing never ending pain.

The Day You Left

The day you left this world.
My world fell apart.
The very moment your
Heart stopped beating
Mine began to ache.
I now have an emptiness
That will always be.
Cause a part of me
Is missing.
There day you left this world
A part of me did to.
With just the blink of an eye
My world was forever changed
Never to be the same4

The Worst Weapons in the World

The Worst Weapon In the world
Is owned by everyone
The damage it causes
Can never be undone
The damage it does
Lingers for all eternity
Keeps causing
Never ending pain
The wounds it causes
Never truly heal
They linger for all
Eternity
When you think the
Damage is gone
It sneaks back in
Like a whisper in your ear
A reminder for you
Saying hey I'm still here
Always causing
Never ending pain
The worst weapon in the world
Is not what you think
It's sharper than any blade
And cuts straight to the heart
It's quicker than any gun
Causing just as much pain

The Worst Weapon In The World is
Words
They cut deep
Cause they sharp
They quicker than
Any gun
Cause they fire back
Before you know it
By then the damage
Is already done

Verbal, Mental and Emotional Abuse

They have several different types of abuse. Some say that the worst type of abuse is physical.
But in my opinion, the worst types of abuse are these 3.

1. Verbal   2) mental and   3) emotional
Growing up there was always talk about physical abuse.
Very seldom did you hear about any other kind of abuse.
Now I am not saying that physical abuse is not bad.
Because it is. But physical abuse
causes wounds and broken bones for everyone to see.
Wounds and broken bones will heal in time.
While verbal, mental, and emotional abuse causes wounds and scars no one can see.
These types of abuse not only attacks their victim's as a person but these types also attacks their victim's mind.
Their victim's way of thinking.
They have away of breaking their victim's mind, heart, soul, and spirit.
No one see's the wound's they cause.
No one see's the scar's they leave behind.
These types of abuse cut deep. These types of abuse leaves wounds that truly never heal. They cause wounds that are there for eternity.
Their victim's suffer for years after the heart aches and pain are gone.
If their victims are lucky enough to get away,
they will still never be the same.
They will be haunted by what they have been through.

I have always said" a broken bone will heal… but a broken mind never does."

You can make a doctor's appointment for a broken bone.

While no doctor can fix a broken mind.

For those lucky enough to get away before permanent damage is done.

Congratulations! May you find piece and happiness.

Some of us did not know all the signs of abuse

Until years later. By then the damage that was done was permanent.

The damage done by these types of abuse can not be undone.

After years of these kinds of abuse. Their victim's mind is broken.

Their victim's will not ever be the same.

These types of abuse leaves their victim's

"TRAGICALLY BROKEN".

For the victim's of these types of abuse let me say;

Try to remember It's not your fault.

You did not ask to be abused.

You are not the blame. It's not your fault you are broken.

The one who abused you in these 3 ways is at fault.

Even though your abuser will try and make you believe it's your fault.

Try to remember. You did not ask for that to happen to you. You are the victim.

The abuser is the one at fault. The abuser and no one else.

In some cases these types of abuse start happening before their victim knows what is really going on.

Inn some cases their victim is young when the abuse starts.

They probably don't even know it's abuse when it starts.

By the time they realize it's abuse the damage is already done.

Once your mind is broken; you will never be the same.

Once people realize you are not the same. They do not want you around.

They do not know how to handle the broken you.

So instead of trying to understand the broken you. They just push you away.

For some it is just easier for you to be out of sight.

Once you are out of sight; then you are out of mind.

I always put it like this. "Outta sight ..Outta mind"

If you not around then they do not see you so they do not think of you.

Therefore they do not have to be around you.

Try to remember that is not your fault either. It is the it's.

It's on them because they do not know how to handle the broken you.

Most won't even try to understand why you are broken.

So try to understand, that none of this is your fault.

You are not the reason you are BROKEN. You are not the blame.

You are not the reason you will never be the same.

You are the victim

Words from Anger

When you are angry
Watch what you say
Cause the things you say
Cuts right thru the heart
Where they will always remain
Because all the sorry's
And all the I didn't mean it's
Won't fix the pain
Caused by your
Spoken angry words
Those spoken words
From Anger
Will always remain
Causing the worst pain

You Will Know

When Your heart is broken
You will forever be changed
No matter what causes
Your broken heart
You will never be the same
The say time will heal
Your plain
But time only teaches you
How to hide the pain
And sometimes how to deal with
The pain
Only you will know
When your heart is whole
Only you will know
When there is no more
Pain

Your Wings

When you left this world
I knew you was ready.
You didn't want to go
You knew I would be alone
But we both knew
There was nothing we could do
Your wings were ready
Even though my heart was not

What Do You See?

Have you ever looked in a mirror
Then asked"what do you see when you look at me?"
You won't believe what I see.
What I see is a little girl
Scared beyond belief.
Scared because she watched her world
Crumble to her feet.
Although a teenager now
The question still remains
"What do you see when you look at me?"
A girl in pain.
Pain from being hurt at a young age.
A girl trying to be brave
Hiding all her hurt and pain
Someone who grew up to soon.
Someone who feels lost and lonely
With nowhere to turn.
Now a young lady
The question still remains.
What do you see when you look at me?
A women who is afraid.
Afraid to let others in
Afraid they too will cause her pain.
She hides her feelings so no one knows
She decided long ago if no one gets close
They can not cause her any pain
Everyone wonders why she is not the same.
But no one knows of her hurt and pain.
Everyone just knows she is no longer the same
Now they know she won't ever be the same again.

The Day

The Day you left this earth.
The very moment everything
Changed forever.
The Day your heart stopped
beating and mine began to hurt.
The Day your eyes closed
forever mined filled with tears.
The Day you left this earth.
That was the day my life was
Forever Changed.
And now I will never be the same

The Worst Kind of Abuse

Verbal and mental abuse causes the worst kind of damage
Damage that will haunt their victims for eternity.
The kind of damage that is deep. The kind that will always remain.
You can not run away from it.
You can not make it leave.
You will constantly hear all those mean cruel and hurtful
things you were told.
For years. after the abuse.
This kind of damage never heals